BOA EDITIONS LTD

Mihyar of Damascus, His Songs

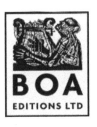

لغةُ الخطيئة

أصرُّ مسيطراً أني أقولُ : أرضى
بلمحٍ ، ولا خبورَ في شبابي
أعبرُ فوق اللهِ والشيطانِ
أدري أنا أبعدُ من دروبِ (الآلة)
والشيطانِ

أعبرُ في كتابي
في مواكبِ الصابغةِ المعصيةِ
في مواكبِ الصابغةِ الخضراءِ
أرضى : لا جنةَ ، لا سقوطَ
بعدي ، وأمحو لغةَ الخطيئة .

Mihyar of Damascus, His Songs

Poems by

Adonis
(Ali Ahmad Sa'id)

Translated from the Arabic by
Adnan Haydar and Michael Beard

BOA Editions, Ltd. ❧ Rochester, NY ❧ 2008

First Edition
08 09 10 11 7 6 5 4 3 2 1

For information about permission to reuse any material from this book please contact The Permissions Company at www.permissionscompany.com or e-mail permdude@eclipse.net.

Publications and programs by BOA Editions, Ltd.—a not-for-profit corporation under section 501 (c) (3) of the United States Internal Revenue Code—are made possible with the assistance of grants from the Literature Program of the New York State Council on the Arts; the Literature Program of the National Endowment for the Arts; the County of Monroe, NY; the Lannan Foundation for support of the Lannan Translations Selection Series; the Sonia Raiziss Giop Charitable Foundation; the Mary S. Mulligan Charitable Trust; the Rochester Area Community Foundation; the Arts & Cultural Council for Greater Rochester; the Steeple-Jack Fund; the Ames-Amzalak Memorial Trust in memory of Henry Ames, Semon Amzalak and Dan Amzalak; and contributions from many individuals nationwide.

Cover Design: Lisa Mauro
Cover Art: Kamal Boullata
Interior Design and Composition: Richard Foerster

BOA Logo: Mirko

Library of Congress Cataloging-in-Publication Data

Adonis, 1930-
  [Aghani Mihyar al-Dimashqi. English]
  Mihyar of Damascus, his songs / by Adonis (Ali Ahmad Sa'id) ; trans. Adnan Haydar and Michael Beard. — 1st ed.
      p. cm. — (Lannan translations selection series no. 12)
    ISBN 978-1-934414-08-8 (pbk. : alk. paper) — ISBN 978-1-934414-09-5 (hardcover : alk. paper)
    I. Haydar, Adnan. II. Beard, Michael, 1944- III. Title.

PJ7862.S519A6513 2007
892.7'16--dc22

2007039116

BOA Editions, Ltd.
Nora A. Jones, Executive Director/Publisher
Thom Ward, Editor/Production
Peter Conners, Editor/Marketing
Glenn William, BOA Board Chair
A. Poulin, Jr., Founder (1938—1996)
250 North Goodman Street, Suite 306
Rochester, NY 14607
www.boaeditions.org

TO SAMUEL HAZO

❧ Contents

III. THE DEAD GOD

IV. IRAM OF THE PILLARS

V. THESE PETTY TIMES

The poetry of Adonis, the pen name of Ali Ahmad Sa'id (b. 1930), elicits superlatives. If the discussion leads to his relationship with the past, the predecessor whose name comes up first is generally al-Mutanabbî (915–65 CE), the monumental figure whose imagery and mastery of sound effects are known for their luminosity, intensity, and surprise. Even treatments of Adonis's biography are marked by big gestures. For example, a story recounted in Samuel Hazo's collection, *Blood of Adonis* (University of Pittsburgh Press, 1971), describes the young Adonis in primary school in Syria, reciting his poetry to a visiting dignitary, including in it a request for support in his education. The story continues that the poem was successful. Future biographers will have no trouble finding memorable vignettes of all kinds. One of the translators of this collection remembers hearing Adonis read from his poetry in the classical mode in villages of north Lebanon as a spokesperson for Al-Hizb al-Sûrî al-qawmî al-ijtimâ'î, the P.P.S.—The Parti Politique Sirien. When, as an established poet, he earned a doctorate at St. Joseph's University in Beirut, his oral examination was televised. He came to the attention of English-speaking readers when various translations began to appear in the early 1970s. Over the last several years he has been a candidate for the Nobel Prize in Literature.

Tracing the stylistic evolution of his poems can evoke a similar vista of superlatives. The poems in this collection, *Mihyar of Damascus, His Songs* (*Aghânî Mihyâr al-Dimashqî* [Beirut: Dâr al-'Awda, 1961]) established a new direction in Arabic poetry, comparable to that series of breaks with traditional styles we find elsewhere at early moments in the history of modernisms: Mallarmé or Apollinaire in France, Ezra Pound in the Anglophone world, Ungaretti in Italy, Sikelianos or Seferis in Greece. Adonis's early poems in traditional metrics demonstrate his mastery of recurring rhythms and monorhyme, but the variations in *Mihyar* shattered that. The authoritative aesthetic break carried out in this book is a break from within. After *Mihyar* there would be many additional leaps into experimental new forms. *Waqt bayna al-ramâd wa al-ward* (1970, expanded in 1972; translated into English by Shawkat M. Toorawa as *A Time Between Ashes and Roses* [Syracuse University Press, 2004]) took his poetry in an explicitly political direction. *Mufrad bi-sîghat al-jam'* (*Singular in plural form* [Beirut: Dâr al-'Awda, 1977]), in which words are scattered across the page in the manner of Mallarmé's "Un coup de dés," generating a pictorial force no less powerful than their sound, explored a whole other aesthetic dimension. More recently, *Al-Kitâb* (The book [London: Dâr al-Sâqî, 1995, followed by a second volume in 1998]) takes the form of a poem, in the center of the page, flanked by marginal comments on it in prose by fictional critics, going down the page in dialogue. *Al-Kitâb* may be Adonis's most striking recent creation, but the poems of *Mihyar* constitute the initial, definitive disruption.

Adonis took on that striking pen name as one of the Tâmmûzî poets, a group named after the dying god Tammûz, whose members contributed to the journal *Shi'r* (Poetry, founded 1957). Readers of Frazer's *Golden Bough* are familiar, as are Syrians and Lebanese of Adonis's generation, with the early mythologies of the Mediterranean: those narratives of gods whose deaths and resurrections define our most persistent narrative patterns. Tammûz, Ishtar, the poet's namesake Adonis, even Jesus who appears occasionally in these poems, provide an underlying narrative that informs the entire sequence.

The particular individual turn that vision takes in Adonis's hand can be seen through his creation of the alter ego Mihyar. The allusion sends us to the early eleventh-century figure, Mihyar of Daylam (in Iran), a convert from Zoroastrianism to Shi'i Islam in 428 AH/1037 CE. (Adonis comes from a Syrian Alawite tradition.) Mihyar was considered the last major poet before a decline in Arabic poetry, and an accomplished elegist. (Note how this collection ends, in a series of elegies.) Even otherwise unsympathetic Sunni observers, writing from across the religious divide, who considered Mihyar of Daylam's conversion a relocation from one corner of hell to another, admired his verse. Adonis invites us to imagine a comparable Mihyar living far to the west in Damascus, in an alternate path of history. The historical Mihyar was indeed a poet, but he does not represent Adonis's poetic tradition. What makes him an appropriate alter ego is that Mihyar of Daylam launched a rebellious voice within the political and religious culture, making him one of those who stood far enough outside the tradition to ensure its dynamism. Similarly, in a three-volume anthology of Arabic poetry that Adonis published between 1964 and 1968, he emphasized poets who altered tradition, particularly poets from the "decadent" seventeenth, eighteenth and nineteenth centuries).

The name Mihyar is not Arabic in its etymology. *Mih-* or *meh-* in Persian is a common prefix for "good" or "well." *Yâr*, a word for "helper," is visible in Persian and Arabic names such as the king Shahrayar in *The Thousand and One Nights*. Once located, as here, in an Arabic context, the name Mihyar looks as if it might have derived from an Arabic word, *inhiyâr*, "to collapse," from the stem *h-w-r*. Indeed, in colloquial eastern Arabic there is a form *mihyâr*—or *mihwâr*—which means a precipice or an abyss. The word Mihyar may not sound to us like a proper noun at all, but, rather, a concept in the construction of Adonis's aesthetic system.

We have spoken of big gestures, but we should add that these poems are delicate in texture, nuanced and precise in ways we may not associate with big gestures. For Adonis's Mihyar there exists no traditional, unified narrative, no series of adventures like those we find in the Fisher-king cycle in Jesse Weston's *From Ritual to Romance* or the Orc cycle in Blake. In the third poem of this collection, we hear the name Mihyar for the first time and realize immediately how concentrated storytelling can be. The poem opens:

> *Malikun Mihyâr*
> *malikun wa-l-hilm lahu qasrun wa hadâ'iqu nâr.*

> Mihyar is king,
> a king whose dreams are palaces
> meadows aflame. . . .

In that opening line, *Malikun Mihyâr* ("a king Mihyar"), the emphasis is on "king," the predicate *malikun* coming first in an emphatic syntactic inversion, which is then restated. Immediately thereafter we learn that the kingdom is in his dreams; hence, "king" begins to look like a figurative term. The third and fourth lines complete the transition:

> *wa-l-yawma shakâhu li-l-kalimât*
> *sawtun mât.*

> [Literally, "and today—complained of him—to words— / a voice (that) died."]

The character we saw as king is now the subject of a complaint. As a narrative, this fits the category of the powerful falling from high places, though the closer we look the less a narrative it seems, since our subject is the speech act. Such linguistic patterns create difficulties for any translator. The Arabic sentence has a telegraphic brevity impossible to reproduce in English syntax. In the preceding excerpt, for example, the verb "complained" (*shakâ*) precedes not only the object (*hu*, referring to Mihyar) and indirect object (*kalimât*, "words") but also the subject (*sawtun*, "a voice")—which is delayed just as the name Mihyar was in the opening line. In our translation we felt obliged to change the verb in order to get the other elements in place:

> Just today, words
> heard complaints against him
> from a voice that died.

Simply put, in Adonis's Mihyar poems the *expression* of the narrative is itself the narrative. We speak of sound and sense as separate entities; we speak of poetry as the place where they cooperate. This scenario, where a voice complains of its own death, to words, about Mihyar, seems a fundamental statement of the values and risks of writing lyric poetry. Mihyar is not so much a character whose actions are described via language as a character located in the machinery of language. To talk about Mihyar is to discuss what poetry can do.

It is one thing for a poem to represent the relation of voice to meaning, of signifier to signified, but the sounds of this poem go further, to offer us one more dimension of the untranslatable. *Kalimât*, words (plural of *kalima*), contains the sound *kalm*, "wound" (plural *kulûm* or *kilâm*) and *mât*, "he died." The echo of that sound in the next line, *sawtun mât*, "a voice [that] died," molds a verse so efficient it may be impossible to hear all its layers at once. It's not lyrical in the way that some of Adonis's verses are lyrical, gradually unfolding or musical ("Bridge of Tears," for instance, or "The Wound"). It is energetic and compact. How could one exit from a statement so intense?

> *Malikun Mihyâr.*
> *Yahyâ fî malakûti-r-rîhi*
> *wa yamluku fî ardi l-asrâr.*
>
> Mihyar, a king.
> He lives in the dominion of the wind
> and rules in the land of secrets.

Yahyâ, "he lives," is a fitting complement to *mât*, "it died." *Malakût*, "kingdom," a word also used to describe heaven or mystical states of the highest level, comes in this context as an elegant transposition of the consonants in *kalimât*, and because it is a kingdom of *rîh*, of wind, we have doubled back to another vision of insubstantiality. If we were to list the contrasts that organize this poem, death and life, success and failure, we would find another twist. The unlikely pair, *ard al-asrâr*, the land of secrets, makes us feel a variation around still another axis, with the concrete feel of *ard*, "land," balancing the abstract notion of *malakût*, "kingdom."

Mihyar was accused of separating voice from words in that early poem. In subsequent poems the reader will find him playing more adventurous roles, albeit intermittently. If it is a narrative we want, we will find it in the gravitational pull between Mihyar and the speaker, a tension that defines the drift of this collection. Although the poems give us only fragments of a narrative, there are stable reference points that create limited cohesion.

Each of the first six sections begins with a prose poem entitled *mazmûr*, a psalm. The psalms suggest the theme of each section. For example, the psalm that begins "The Knight of Strange Words" describes a Mihyar-like character in the third person, whereas in the second psalm, for "The Sorcerer of Dust," the voice switches to a first-person account of a paradoxical state that combines death and life. From Knight to Sorcerer to the late, departed god in the third section, those overtures establish a sense of closure, if not of resolution. In the psalm for the section entitled "Iram of the Pillars," Adonis announces an explicit theme for the forthcoming poems, satires, and wry commentaries: "My country and I tease one another," the psalm begins. The psalm structure leads us to notice how the poems are linked thematically: how, for instance, one poem on a figure from Greek mythology (Orpheus) towards the middle of "The Sorcerer of Dust" leads to others (Odysseus, Sisyphus) continuing that theme.

In "Barbarian Saint," the poem that concludes "The Knight of Strange Words," we get a hint of the future unspoken merger between Mihyar and the speaker, and there is even a term that will recur as the title of the fifth section, "petty times." (A variation of the same term will show up in "The Wound," the poem that sets the tone for "The Sorcerer of Dust.") The poems stand alone, as Adonis's many anthology pieces demonstrate. Still, it is useful to translate an entire collection to give the reader a chance to see the act of creation, the constant improvisation of different, expanding meanings as Adonis's vision unfolds.

When we speak of a poet finding the right voice, the discovery forces us to look at individual poems. (Where else would it happen?) On the other hand, the organizing principles can be so complex that important elements become visible only as we draw back to look at the collection as a whole. We may feel at some point that we are seeing a separate act of creation outside that of any individual poem. Elements of the Mihyar poems (the tight arc of his birth, death and transformations, his absorption by the speaker) allow him to combine figures of exaggeration with a characteristic precision and refinement. Discordant elements combine to establish strategies that become familiar to us—as linguistic rules become second nature to children learning their own languages.

Adonis's characteristic vocabulary is an important aspect of this process. We do not have to read far in *Mihyar* to begin noticing privileged terms: *jaras* (bell), *jamr* (ember), *hajar* (stone) and its inexact synonym *sakhra* (which we translate as "rock"), *hâwiya* (abyss, precipice) and *ghubâr* (dust), including body parts (*jufûn*, eyelids; *wajh*, face; *ahdâf*, eyelashes) and weather (*rîh*, wind; *sâ'iqa*, thunderbolt; *ghuyûm*, clouds). It is possible to imagine a repetition of terms that made their use more precise, but here repetition engenders opacity, a place on the page where we attend to sound first. Ironically, they may be the moments when translation has the least difficulty since if the word is opaque it is opaque in either language. The metamorphosis of the word "wound" in the poem by that name ("Jurh") forces our attention to this rhythmic device:

> Leaves, asleep under wind:
> a ship for the wound.
> The wound
> glories in these ruinous times.
> Trees growing in our own eyelashes
> a lake for the wound.
> The wound shows up in bridges
> as graves reach out
> as patience wears thin on the opposite banks
> between our love and our death.
> And the wound, a beckoning gesture,
> inflicts us as we cross.

It is one of the many ways Adonis manages to make the location of repeated images as important as their dictionary meanings.

Sometimes the key words are elemental—stone, tree, wind—and sometimes Adonis will privilege a term that seems less consequential and significant, such as the flag in "King over the Winds":

> *Tarafun râyatî lâ tu'âkhî wa lâ tatalâqâ*
> *tarafun ughniyâtî . . .*

> [Literally, "A side/a margin, my banner/flag doesn't fraternize, doesn't meet (with anyone). / A side, my songs."]

Here is another dilemma. The poem seems to say, with *tarafun râyatî*, that my flag or banner (*râya*) has a commitment, a *taraf*—a side or "position." The two negatives that follow push in the other direction: *lâ tu'âkhî*, "it doesn't fraternize" and *lâ tatalâqâ*, "it doesn't meet (with anyone)." It was in the first psalm, "The Knight of Strange Words," that the heroic figure showed *taqâtu' al-atrâf*, how "extremities converge," where *atrâf*, the plural of *taraf* represents the many discordant pairs that come together in the poems. To confirm that you belong to a *taraf* is to take sides, as a banner or flag will show an affiliation or a nationality.

The core statement *tarafun râyatî* leads us towards many meanings. In Arabic, *râya* (flag) is associated with both *ra'a* (to see, observe, behold) and *ra'yun* (an opinion, conception, viewpoint). *Mirâya* (mirror) and *ru'yâ* (vision) stem from the same tree of meanings. In this respect it is like the words for signs and signification in English, which trace back to Latin *signum*, a flag or banner. This is a poem, then, about the processes of meaning, about commitment to one's aesthetics:

> My flag takes sides
> with no fraternal pact.
> It flutters alone,
> my songs a faction in themselves.

What Adonis accomplishes is a language so attentive to its contexts and inner pressures that he allows the nuances to unfurl. The poem concludes:

> Here I am launching the stars and fastening them down,
> proclaiming myself king over the winds.

As king of the winds he makes us notice not anything written on the flag but the forces of nature flowing over it.

We have come to love that moment when the statement of the poem repositions itself, when a shift in vision allows us to see the context that holds the statement in place. This shift of perspective from the message to the mechanisms of language that make a message possible is characteristic of Adonis, and for us that movement of surprise, that shock as the camera moves back, is one of the great pleasures of reading his poetry.

—Adnan Haydar & Michael Beard

MIHYAR OF DAMASCUS, HIS SONGS

"O beautiful sun, why aren't you enough for me?"
of a sudden he comes to wake us up,
the strange one,
the sound that creates people.
> —Hölderlin

(بلادي القديمة)

أَسْلَمْتُ للصُّخورِ والأصْداء
رَايَاتِيَ المَهْزُومَةَ النِّداء

أَسْلَمْتُكِ بَلْغَةَ الغُبار
كِبرِياءَ الرَّفضِ والهَزِيمَة .

لَمْ يَبْقَ لي ... يا بلادي القديمة
أُبَشِّرُ الأشرار .

I. THE KNIGHT OF STRANGE WORDS

Psalm

He arrives unarmed, a forest, a cloud not to be warded off. Yesterday he lifted up a continent and moved the sea from its place.

He draws the back side of day. He fashions a day from his feet. He borrows night's shoes and waits for what will not come. He is the physics of things—he knows them and he calls them by names he will not disclose. He is reality and its contrary, life and its other.

Where stone becomes lake, where shadow becomes city, he lives: he lives on and frustrates despair, erasing the empty spaces of hope, dancing for the soil until it yawns, dancing the trees to sleep.

Here he is, showing how extremities converge, chiseling on the brow of our time the magic spell.

No one sees him, though his presence fills life. He churns it into foam and dives in. He transforms tomorrow into his prey and runs behind it in despair. Engraved, his echoing words: they fade out into loss loss loss.

Indecision is his homeland—for all his store of eyes.

He terrifies. He gladdens.

Disaster oozes through him. He overflows with scorn.

He peels man like an onion.

He is wind. The wind does not retrace its steps. He is water. Water never flows back to its source. He creates his own kind. Starting with himself. He has no ancestors. His roots are in his footsteps.

He stalks the abyss, his stature like the wind.

Neither a Star

Neither a star
nor a breath of prophecy.
Nor is he a face
humbled before the moon.

Here he comes. A barbarian spear
sweeping across the land of letters.
Bleeding, he exposes his blood to the sun.

Lo, he wears the nakedness of stone,
offering to caves his prayers.

And lo, he gathers to himself the pliant land.

∽ Mihyar Becomes King

Mihyar is king,
a king whose dreams are palaces
meadows aflame.

Just today, words
heard complaints against him
from a voice that died.

Mihyar, a king.
He lives in the dominion of the wind
and rules in the land of secrets.

∽ His Voice

Mihyar: a face
betrayed by its lovers.
Mihyar: bells that don't ring.
Mihyar: it's written on our faces—
a song that sneaks up on us
through the white paths of his exile.
Mihyar
a church bell for passersby
lost in this Galilean land.

Another Voice

He lost the thread of things. His inner star
went out. He never stumbled.

When his wanderings turned to stone
and boredom hollowed his cheeks,
slowly he assembled his remains
to breathe life into them
assembled them and fell apart.

Birth of Eyes

In the rock's dizzy tumbling
you search for Sisyphus.
His eyes spring to life,

spring to life
among the many eyes
bewildered, lusterless,
calling for Ariadne.

His eyes spring to life
in a voyage meandering like blood
that flows from the dead body of space.

In a world wearing the face of death
(impregnable to language and to sound)
those eyes again.

The Days

His eyes have tired of days
have tired regardless of days.
Must he burrow
through wall after wall
of days
just to find another day?
Is there another day
somewhere?

Death Call (Voices 1)

Mihyar batters us
he burns away our life's outward skin
and our patience. He burns away
our peaceable features.

So surrender to horror and calamity,
land of our fathers,
you, bride of God, of tyrants,
and give in to his fire.

Voice

Between rock and oar he disembarks.
Inside wedding jars
he joins with wandering souls.
He violates the oyster's secret thoughts.

Then he proclaims the rebirth of our roots,
of seaports, singers, and wedding songs,
proclaims the resurrection of the seas.

⤞ Mask of Songs

In the name of his own history,
in a country mired in mud,
when hunger overtakes him
he eats his own forehead.
He dies.
The seasons never find out how.
He dies behind the interminable mask of songs.

The only loyal seed,
he dwells alone buried deep in life itself.

⤞ In the City of the Partisans

I.
Open your arms
O city of partisans.
Welcome him with thorns
or with stones.
Bind his arms above his head,
stretch them into an archway to the grave,
tattoo upon his head
graven images, brand him with glowing coals
and let the flames consume Mihyar.

II.
More than an olive tree, more
than a river, more than
a breeze
bounding and rebounding,
more than an island
more than a forest,
a cloud
that skims across his leisurely path:

all and more
in their solitude
are reading his book.

New Testament

He doesn't speak this language.
He doesn't know the voices of the wastes.
A soothsayer in stony sleep
he is burdened with distant languages.

Here he comes from under the ruins
in the climate of new words,

offering his poems to grieving winds
unpolished but bewitching like brass.

He is a language glistening between the masts
the knight of strange words.

Between Echo and Call

Between echo and call he hides.
He hides under the iciness of letters.
In the longing of wanderers he hides,
hides in the waves, between seashells.

When morning's shutters close
upon his eyes
and darkness hides him,
he finds the mountain
his despair had lost,
shelters his lamp in it
then himself.

Bell

The palm trees bow
the day bows.
Evening too.
He's coming. He is like us

except that
in the power of his name
the sky doffed its rainy ceiling
and came closer
to suspend his face above us
a green bell.

Where the Sky Ends

He dreams of throwing his eyes
into the heart of the city that will be,
of forgetting his days
days that devour things
and the days that create things.

He dreams of rising and collapsing

like the sea. He crowds the realm of secrets,
starting his sky
where the sky ends.

Mihyar's Face

Mihyar's face:
a fire that burns the land
of tame stars.

And here he is overstepping
the caliph's boundaries
advancing the flag
of retreat,
destroying every home.
Here he is turning down the offer
of leadership,
leaving his despair behind
above the face of seasons.

Indecision (Voices 2)

Because he is of many minds
he taught us how to read the dust.

Because he is of many minds
a cloud charged with his fire
passed over our seas
brimming with the thirst of generations.

Because he is of many minds
imagination willed to us
his pens, passed on to us his book.

He Sleeps in His Own Arms

He stretches out his palm
to the dead homeland
to mute streets,

and when death fastens itself
to his eyes
he wears the earth's skin

the skin of objects.
He sleeps in his own arms.

He Carries in His Eyes

He takes a gleam from his eyes.
From wind's last breath
from the edge of time
he takes a spark.
And from the island of the rain
he takes their substance
and creates the dawn.

I know him. He carries in his eyes
the prophecy of the seas.
He named me History, the poem
that washes all space clean.

I know him. He called me the great flood.

Day's Twin

The night is made of doors and witches.
Mihyar breathes them in,
into his yellowing face, into his hands.

Die like us. Be lost, like us
O Adam of life.
Sail with us to him.
We yearn for him, we live for him
Mihyar.
He is our double, day's twin.

The Others

Knowing them,
he threw a rock
over their heads.
He turned away
carrying the blaze on day's forehead
and carrying the fleeting, virgin years
each big with child.

His face feels
the tug of strange frontiers.
He bends over them
glowing with his own light.

He comes to a place
where no one meets him
but himself.
Where he sees no one
he turns around
carrying the blaze on day's forehead,
erasing the pages of familiar skies.

Barbarian Saint

There he is. Mihyar, your barbarian saint—
O country of visions, of longing,
there he is, armed with my forehead,
wearing my lips,
advancing against petty times,
closed to passers by.

There's Mihyar, your barbarian saint—
under his fingernails,
blood and a god.

He is the mischievous creator.
His loved ones are those who saw him
and were lost.

أيّتها الميّت فوق الخشبة

يا حبيبتي

سمعت وتهيّأت أزهار الطريق

ومشيت تطفئ

نظرات العيون .

II. THE SORCERER OF DUST

∽ *Psalm*

Carrying my abyss, I sally forth. I efface the lines of endless roads, open them out as easily as air, as dust. With every footstep I make my enemies emerge, enemies worth fighting against. The abyss shapes itself into a pillow. The ruins intercede on my behalf.

Verily I am death in person.

Memorials are my trademark. I make erasures and wait for someone to erase me. My smoke and magic work without the slightest impediment. In such a guise I inhabit the wind's memory.

I am discovering the voice, the idiom of our age and its complaints—

(An age that crumbles like sand, and like zinc solidifies. It is the age of clouds. We call them herds. The age of empty slates called brains. It is the age of submission, of mirage, the age of the doll, the scarecrow, the age of the gluttonous moment, the age of bottomless decline.)

Lacking even a single artery to connect me with this age, I am dismantled. Nothing can put me back together.

I create a desire like the panting of a dragon.

I live, concealed in the lap of a returning sun. I find refuge in night's childhood, leaving my head on the morning's knees. I exit, writing the chapters of my exodus, though no promised land awaits.

I am both a prophet and a doubter.

I knead the rising dough of fallen time, then leave the past to its fallen self. I choose to be myself. Flattening current time, I roll it into armor. I call out, "Dwarf giant, giant dwarf"—I laugh, I cry.

I am a proof against the times.

I erase the traces and the stains inside me. I wash my inner self. I keep it empty, clean. Thus I live, within myself.

When I bleed, my veins refill with blood. There's no place for me among the dead. Life is my victim and I don't know what it is to die. Though eyes are everywhere, my time is hidden: yesterday I swam into the ritual of waves and water was my flame.

I am in a hurry. Death's winds follow me, crowding my eyes. We laugh together and with the tenderness of eyelashes I cry—death the laughing, crying one.

I know I am in the prime of death. I mumble through my nose. I enter the grave's belly. But I'm alive. The others know this. Not me.

I attack and uproot. I cross over and I mock. Where I pass by a cascade falls from another world. Where I pass by there is death and no passageway.

I intend to remain. Barricaded by my self.

❧ The Wound

I.

Leaves, asleep under wind:
a ship for the wound.
The wound
glories in these ruinous times.
Trees growing in our own eyelashes
a lake for the wound.
The wound shows up in bridges
as graves reach out
as patience wears thin on the opposite banks
between our love and our death.
And the wound, a beckoning gesture,
inflicts us as we cross.

II.

And to that language
in which the bell sound chokes
I confer the voice of the wound.
For the stone, approaching
this withered world from afar,
for the act of withering
for these slippery times
carried skidding on their sleighs
I light the wound's fire.

As history smolders in my clothes,
as blue claws spread across my book,
as I cry out at the day

"Who are you? Who throws you
across these pages
in my virgin land?"
that's when in my pages I glimpse
in that land two eyes of dust.
I hear one saying
"I am he, the wound
that grows bigger
in your petty little history."

III.
I called you clouds,
you my wound, my migrating dove.
I called you feather
called you book
and here we are
where the dialogue between me
and a deeply rooted language begins.
We meet in the storied isles
on failure's deeply rooted archipelago.
And here I am
teaching this dialogue
to wind and palm tree,
to you my wound
you migrating dove.

IV.
If only the land of dreams and mirrors
had seaports,
if only I had a ship,
or the remnants of a city.
If only I possessed a city
in the land of children,
that land of lamentation,
I'd recast it all in ingots
so that the wound, molded into song,
could cut like a lance

that pierces trees, rocks, and sky,
a song supple like water,
as defiant and perplexed
as conquest.

V.
Rain upon our desert
O world decked with dream and longing.
Rain down enough to shake us.
We are the wound's palm trees.
From those trees captivated by the wound's silence,
trees which nursed the wound
through its night,
among arches of eyelashes and arms bent with care
break off for us just two branches.

O world decked in dream and longing
O world that falls onto my forehead
etched like a wound,
keep your distance. The wound is closer than you.
Keep your seductive charms away. More beautiful than you
is the wound.
And the magic that reaches
from your eyes
to the last kingdoms
has only been the wound's pathway.
The wound has passed over it,
stripped it of its deceptive sails
and left it without its island.

A God Has Died

There was a god there
who died
falling from the sky's skull.

Perhaps in fear, in calamity
in despair, in loss
that god will rise
from inside me.

May earth be a bed for me
a wife
a gentle bend in my path.

∝ *Loss*

I lose my way
I throw my face
at the midday and its dust.
I throw my face
at madness.
My eyes are made of grass and fire,
of banners and people leaving.

I lose my way. I throw
my face at midday
and its dust.
At the end of the road
I behold my birth.
I shout—Let the road and dust shout out with me:

Good God how beautiful for my face
to lose its way
and thus be free of me,
for me to lose my way
brimming with fire.

Dear Grave: you mark where I end
and spring begins.

Stone

I worship this gentle stone.
I've seen my face in it,
my own lost poems.

The Fall

Between fire and plague
we live
my language and I
within these mute worlds.
I live in the apple garden and in the sky,
in the first joy, the first sadness
between Eve's arms.
I live as master of the cursed trees,
the master of their fruits.

I live between the clouds and their crackling sparks
inside a stone, growing
inside a book, revealing
secrets, explaining the fall.

Dialogue

"Who are you? Who do you choose, Mihyar?
Wherever you turn
There is either God or Satan's precipice.
As one hell goes by, another takes its place.
The world is a question of choice."

"Neither God nor Satan will I choose.
Both are impenetrable walls.
Both shut my eyes to the light.

Shall I just trade one wall for another?
For mine is the perplexity of the unknowing
and my confusion is the confusion
of one who gives off light,
the perplexity of the all-knowing."

❧ The Language of Sin

I burn my inheritance.
I say my land
is still untilled. No graves
disturb my youth.
From farther than God
or the Devil I set out.
(My path rises farther than God's
or Satan's.)

I pass across my book
in a procession of glowing thunderbolts,
a procession of green thunderbolts.
I cry out with joy
"There is neither paradise
nor a fall after me."
With that I erase the language of sin.

❧ King over the Winds

My flag takes sides
with no fraternal pact.
It flutters alone,
my songs a faction in themselves.

Here I am mobilizing the flowers, enlisting the trees.
The sky I redesign in colonnades.
I experience love. I live. I'm born into words.

Here I am rounding up butterflies
under the auspices of morning.

I nurture the fruits.
We go home for the night, the rain and I,
home in the clouds with their bells, home in the sea.

Here I am launching the stars and fastening them down,
proclaiming myself king over the winds.

The Rock

I give in to your commands: my songs
shall be my bread, my kingdom
words.
So, my rock,
make these steps firm.
Since dawn I've been carrying you on my shoulders.
I've sketched you as a vision on my face.

Precipice

I find myself at a precipice, but how to see it
when I'm afraid to look?
I find myself at a precipice,
charged with the joy of one who warns and promises,
the joy that makes my song
evolve another song
to guide this blinded world,

with the joy of becoming
both sin
and he who
living in innocence
still sins.

With My Own Secrets

I know a secret way to walk
across a spider's web.
I know the secret of living
under the eyelashes of a god who doesn't die.

I am a lover. I live inside my face, inside my voice.
I know a secret way to father new generations
after my death.

Your Eyes Never Saw Me

Your eyes never saw me
innocent as a living drop of sperm.
They never saw me arriving
in the procession of promises
trailing greenery and lightning bolts
wherever I step.

Tomorrow, tomorrow
afire in the green season
you shall know that I am he
who nurtures the seeds.
Tomorrow, tomorrow your eyes
will believe in me.

❧ Dialogue

"Where were you?
What light weeps beneath your eyelashes?
Where were you?
Show me what you've written."

I didn't answer her. I didn't know a single word.
I had to find a star
under the clouds of ink.

"What light weeps beneath your eyelashes?
Where were you?"
I didn't answer her. The night was just a tent—
the lanterns, a tribe,
and I an emaciated sun.
Under that sun the earth changed her contours
and the wanderer found himself
on the long road.

❧ Presence

I open a door into the earth. I light the fire of presence
in clouds that unweave and recombine.
I light it in the ocean with its love-tossed waves
in the mountains with their rocks and forests.

I create a homeland for the pregnant evenings
from the ashes of roots
from meadows made of songs,
from thunder and lightning.

The mummies of time I consign to fire.

The Seven Days

Mother, who makes light of me
whether I love or hate,
you were created in seven days.
You gave birth to the waves and the horizons
even the feathers of songs.

And I, my seven days
am but a wound, a crow—
so why the mystery
when I, like you, am only
wind and clay?

Orpheus

I'm a lover, tumbling headlong into the dark of hell,
like a stone, except I give off light.

I have a date with the priestesses
in the old god's bed.
My words: a wind that stirs up life.
My songs: a shower of sparks.

I'm a language for a god who's yet to come,
the sorcerer of dust.

Land of Magic

It's over—no hostilities, no revenge
between us, time's watchman and me.
Everyone passing by has fenced in his history
with clouds. Everyone has seen his own limits.

And yet my land remains a land of wizardry:
I contradict the wind.
I wound the face of water.
I break out of a bottle in the sea.

A Vision

O Babylon of flames, of secrets,
go mask yourself in charred wood.
I am waiting for the god who's on his way
adorned in fire,
decked with stolen pearls,
from oysters the seas breathed out.

I'm waiting for an indecisive god,
prone to anger, who cries, prostrates himself,
and gives off light.

It's your face, Mihyar,
that prophesies the god
who's on his way.

Voyage

I shall ride on a wave, on a wing,
visit the ages that abandoned us,
visit the seventh sky,
visit lips,
eyes brimming with snow,
visit the shining blade of God's own hell.

And I shall disappear, strap myself to the winds
and leave my footsteps far behind
where the road divides and mazes begin.

Leave for Us What's Behind You

Go on, go ahead. Embrace the waves and wind.
Carry clouds and lightning in the lashes of your eyes.
Leave behind our broken mirror.
Let the flask that holds the years break too.
Leave for us what's behind you.
No. Don't leave anything behind
except shards of clay and sorrow,
except the dried blood in your veins.

Oh, go ahead. Take your time.
Your sun is about to set. So leave for us what's behind you,
your eyes, your dark corpse, your robe,
as a poem for the strange world,
for the world that comes with yearning,
that carries your sky in its lashes.

I Surrendered My Days

I surrendered my days to a precipice
ground that disappears under my carriage.
I've carved out a grave in my eyes.
I'm the master of ghosts. I bestow my own nature on them.
Yesterday I gave them my language.
I cried over history. When I saw it defeated
and fading away upon my lips
I cried over the horror,
all those green trees charred inside my lungs.
I'm the master of ghosts.
I beat them back,
with my voice, with my own blood. I herd them along.
The sun is just a lark.
I gave it my bow and gave the wind my hat.

Bridge of Tears

There is a bridge of tears walking beside me.
Beneath my eyelids it disintegrates.
Under my fragile skin
a knight of childhood tethers his horses
beneath shadowy branches
with the wind for a rope.
He sings for us with the voice of a prophet:

"O you winds
O childhood
O bridges made of tears
disintegrating behind eyelids."

I Have No Limits

For the sake of my road, dressed in waves and mountains,
for the sake of my face, stocked with echoes,
I snuffed out sky's white candles by the thousands.

I spoke to my teeth, I asked the blue claws
to be flexible and give in to the waves and the roar,
I asked them to cut the ropes
between the last shore and me—

I have no limits, no final shore.

Dams

Every day morning is recited, reread.
Every day these caves under the skin,
these dams, these ruins,

and always these places of refuge.
Always these graves beneath eyelashes,
these dismembered parts, these victims
victims of your songs.
Your face has never had a landscape,
never had a dance or a birth in it.

Always the miscarriage in your veins—
You contain, inside your bark, a star,
inside the rock, your heritage,
inside the day, a whole country
you prince of emptiness,
language into which winds and distances empty.

The Solitary Land

These homeless words are where I live.
I go through life, my face my face's friend,
my face the path I take.
I swear by your name, my land, as you extend
enchanted, solitary,
and Death, my friend, by your name I swear.

Wish

If only a cedar tree seasoned with depth, with years,
would open its embrace to me,
if only it could protect me
from the lure of pearls and sails—

if only I had its roots, if only my face
were anchored behind its sad bark.

Then I might have been the clouds, the shafts of light
winking on the horizon—might have been this trusted land.

But all my life each branch
seasoned with depth, with years,
has lit its fire on my brow,
a fire lit with fever and with loss
consumes the earth that shelters me.

I Said to You

I said to you I listened to the seas.
I heard them read their poems to me. I listened
to the bell that sleeps within the oysters.
I told you I sang
at the devil's wedding,
that banquet of fairy tales.
I told you I saw
in the falling rain of history, in the glare of distance,
I saw a genie and a house.

Because I sail within my eyes
I can tell you I have seen everything
right from the first step I took into the distance.

Defeat

Here I am, my songs, melting you down
to recast you as clouds, as elegy, as rain.
Mixing crime with kindness
I weave the soil's flag,
weave the morning with the spears of defeat.

Magic, fire, banquets
are my kingdom. Fog
is my army—the entire world, defeat.

Enough for You to See

It's enough just to see.
It's enough just to die far away,
embracing the heights.

There is no silence in your eyes, no words.
It's as if you were smoke.
Your skin sheds in one place,
you in another.

It's enough just to live in the maze,
defeated, mute as a nail
without a glimpse of the god on people's foreheads.

Mihyar, it is enough for you
To keep the secret god erased.

Seeing is enough for you.
It's enough for your death to come from far away.

Chair (A Dream)

Long ago I screamed at the city:
Husk of the world,
I'm holding you in my hand.
Long ago I muttered at the ship—
my song in a rose-red blaze:
all or nothing.

As for you, my grandchildren, I'm tired,
tired of myself, tired of the seas.
Bring me that chair.

The Lamp

In full daylight he carries
his lamp. He's looking for someone,
no sand in his eyes.
He walks wearing dust for sandals.
He sleeps in a barrel
his own hands for a bed.

"And you—what about you?"
"I have no eyes.
Between me and my brothers is Abel.
Between me and the other is the flood.

When night and day sleep
I take the murderer by surprise.
I walk and dust walks behind me,
but I walk without a lamp."

I Search for Odysseus

I wander into caves of sulphur
I embrace the sparks.
In clouds of incense, in the talons of afreets
I take their secrets by surprise.

I search for Odysseus,
hoping he might extend his days,
a ladder for me to climb,

hoping he might tell me,
tell me what the waves don't know.

Old Country

I surrendered to the rocks and to the echoes.
I let them have my flags, those choking calls.
I surrendered them to the fortress of dust,
to the arrogance of rejection and defeat.

All I have left is you, my old country,
you, all those secrets.

Land with No Return

Even if you come back, Odysseus,
even if all those distances have hemmed you in,
even if your guide bursts into flame
right before your tragic face
or in your intimate terror

you will still be a whole history of wandering,
still be in an unanticipated land
still in a land with no return,

even if you come back, Odysseus.

Today I Have My Own Language

I destroyed my kingdom.
I destroyed my throne, my public squares, my hallways

and I've started searching. Carried by my lungs,
I teach the sea with my rainstorms, I bestow on it
both my fire and my embers.
Write down the coming times upon my lips.

Today I have my own language.
I have my space, my land, my own features.
I have my people feeding me with their uncertainties.
They get their light from my ruins, from my wings.

✑ *The Earth*

How often you have said to me
"I have another country,"
your palms filling with tears
and your eyes
filling with lightning
from where the borders keep edging closer.

Did your eyes know that the earth,
wherever it cried or it cheered your footsteps,
here where you have sung, or there,
that it knows every passerby but you
and knows itself to be one,
dried up breasts, dry inside,
and that it doesn't know the ritual of rejection?

Did your eyes realize
that you yourself are the earth?

A Language for the Distances

Only yesterday,
I traveled here beneath my eyelids,
the dust floating overhead.
And so I heard our echoes
and heard the boundaries collapsing.

When I got home people said
I had left behind
my own footsteps.
I was so surprised.
My footsteps?
Yes, it's as if I saw them
free, circulating through veins and lungs,
roaming deep inside me, led on
amazed, confused,
in the folds of waists, inside the skin
at a precipice you cannot see.
It's as if I saw them return.

You will pass by,
and you won't notice my footsteps.
Between us, a language for the distances
that no one knows but us.

Lightning

It beckoned to me, cried and went to sleep
in the forest of possibilities.
It didn't know who I was,
didn't know I am the master of darkness.

The lightning beckoned to me, cried and went to sleep.
It slept upon my hands
from the moment it saw my eyes.

My Shadow and the Earth's

Come up close, sky,
and rest in my narrow grave,
on my broad forehead.
Stay as you are, faceless, without hands,
without a breathing sound,
without a pulse,
and paint yourself as two selves,
my shadow and the shadow of the earth.

Odysseus

"Who are you, from what summits
have you come?
O virgin speech that no one knows but you.
What is your name—
what flags have you carried or thrown away?"

Is this what you are asking Alkinoos?
"Alkinoos, do you want to unveil the dead man's face,
to ask from what summits he has come—
to ask 'What is my name?'
My name is Odysseus.
I come from a land without boundaries,
carried on people's backs.
I got lost here. There, I got lost with my poems.
And here I live in terror, all dried up.
I don't know if I'll stay or go back home."

قد تصير بلادي

هآ أنا أتسلّق أصعد فوق صباح بلادي

فوق أنقاضها وذكراها

هآ أنا أتخلّص من ثقل الموت فيّ

هآ أنا أتعرّب عنك

لأراها

فغدا قد تصير بلادي .

III. The Dead God

∽ Psalm

I am the opening of day, and also the last one to arrive—I put my face at the lightning's mouth and tell the dream to be my bread. I hoist the butterfly as my flag. I write my names on it.

A tree changes its name and comes to me. A stone washes itself with my voice. I sprout across plain—these leaves are my armies, grass my weapon.

I engrave my face on the wind and on the stone. I engrave it on water. I inhabit the horizon, and on my brow—a mask of waves.

I head forth, into the distance, and the distance stays in place. This is how I am, without origin. But still I emit light. I have gone far away and that distance is my homeland.

I create a homeland, a friend like tears.

Those who plant their mines under the earth's husk, those who are filled with glowing embers, living next door to the horizon, those who vandalize the horizon, who beat it until it bleeds, those who rest in the shade cast by butterflies.

These I call by my names. I'm the one in motion. When the gods encircle me, I abduct them, I attack them. And as I touch them I wear their funerals like a pair of gloves. I'm the one housed in the dream's seashells, the one announcing an inner man. (Look behind you, Orpheus, learn how to walk around in the world.)

I announce the flood of rejection. I announce its genesis.

I converse with caves and transform mountains into words. I set the earthworks in order. I dance with the air. I charge the stone to deliver my yearnings to the land. I conjure a spell for my days, and I break up the meter that measures time. I mark my distances with dismembered limbs and I let those distances lead me onward.

Stone's Mirror

Naked beneath the palm trees of the gods,
wearing only the sands of passing time
I toyed with my own death.
For the others building kingdoms with my own dust,
I call on you, prophet of lost words,
prophet of voyages coming towards us
in the winds of rain—
Despair and I both knew you were coming.
We knew you as a prophet whose time had arrived.
And so we bowed before you.
We cried out "You who are coming,
lost, immersed in exile and in fire,
we accept you as a god and as a friend
in the mirrors of stone."

You prophet of voyages,
I accept you as a god
a companion in the mirrors of stone.

Today, in your name, I'll sing for the clouds.
Between my heart and the space above,
at the edge of the stars,
I'll build a barrier wearing a human face, a sky.
I will sing for the clouds—
my face is stone and stone is all I worship.

Song

Whether in mute or silenced letters,
perhaps in no voice at all,
perhaps in words beneath the moaning earth,

this is my song to death
to the joy ailing in things, for the sake of things.
This is my song for rejection.

Come to me, words of terror, of healing,
you words of sickness.

One Time Only

For once, for one last time
I dream of falling in place.

I'm living in the island of colors,
living as a man lives.
I reconcile the blind gods with the gods who see

for one last time.

The Second Land

Here I am on my way to my second land
bringing with me my flags and my own winds.

Day dies
pulling behind it daylight's carriages
pulling all those houses.

Confession

Nothing is left but night's corpse
and my dismembered hands

in day's outline,
nothing but a stone under the eyelids.

How often I have prayed to an obstinate god
for his fruits.

Often I've fed my own eyes to the hunger of trees
and walked over my own broken eyelashes
just for an encounter, a pagan embrace—
God and I, and day's ruins.

❧ *Prayer*

I prayed that you would stay buried in the ashes.
I prayed that you would never glimpse the day, never wake up.
We did not experience your night, never sailed through that
    blackness.

I prayed, Phoenix,
that magic would hold still
so we might meet in fire, in ashes.

I prayed that madness would guide us.

❧ *Traveler*

I leave my face behind
on my lamp's glass shade.
My map, a land with no creator.
My bible, rejection.

Thunderbolt

I call on you, green thunderbolt.
I take you as my wife, in sunlight and in madness.
The rock has collapsed on my eyelids
so blast away the map of things.

I come to you from a skyless land,
I'm full of God,
that precipice inside.
From winds, from eagles, I take my wings.
I force seeds into the sand
and bow down to the approaching cloud.

And so I call on you to change the map of things.
You are my image in sunlight and in madness,
my green thunderbolt.

After the Silence

I call upon the silence where words never venture.
I call out: who among you
shapeless fragments, dying
under such silence, can see me?

I call out so winds might give birth
to winds in my voice
so morning turns to language
in my blood and in my songs.

I call out: who among you can see me
inside the silence where words never venture?

I call out to confirm I'm alone—just me and the dark.

The Godly Wolf

Morning—wanderer with a burning face:
while I become the moon's death.

Beneath my face Night's bell is silenced.
I have become the new godly wolf.

Children's Footsteps

Here's your wish: I'll give you the genie and the smoke
you, gray horse
we feed with cactus and with chaff.

I'll give you the winds and the doors.
I'll give you toys,
a dream, yellow notebooks,
the alphabet, writing
in rooms full of wisdom and proverbs.

O sun, you genie seen in waterfall and cloud,
O children's footsteps.

The Thunderbolt's Stone

I am the thunderbolt's stone,
the god who lurks at lost crossroads.
I am the banner hanging
from the eyelids of passing clouds, the sinister rain.

I am the lost one walking ahead of flood and fire
mixing sky and dust.

I speak the dialect of lightning and thunderbolt.

Lost Face

I'm the one with the lost face—I pray for my dust
I sing my exiled soul

to a miracle still incomplete.
Stepping across a world my songs have burned
I lay down a threshold.

I Create a Land

I create a land to revolt with me, to betray me,
a land felt in my veins,
whose skies I etched with my thunder,
decorated with my lightning.

Its boundaries—peals of thunder, waves.
Its flag—my eyelids.

Betrayal

Blessed betrayal,
you world lengthening my footsteps,
a sheer cliff, a fire,
you centuries-old corpse,
world I have betrayed and will again.

I am that drowned being whose eyelids pray
for the sound of tumbling waves.
I am that god
who will bless the crime-laden earth.

I'm a traitor. I sell my existence
to the cursed road.
I am the master of betrayal.

Seashell

Were you scared, Satan? Go change your defeated face.
You are the one who carries me above the stars.
I'm not afraid of the silent road.
I am the wind of the simoom.
I'm like a seashell.
My grave has been dug under my face.

Go ahead—forsake the dreams in your trembling eyelashes
and stay clenched in my throat,
you, Satan, who carries me underneath the stars.

The Dead God

Today I burned up the mirage of Saturday,
the mirage of Friday.
Today, I cast off the house's mask.
I exchanged the god of blind stone,
And the god of the seven days,
for a dead one.

Sacrifice

In the caves of ancient torture
where I loved some god
where I was in love with the palace women

where we lived, me and my friend, madness—
lost—from one month to the next.
So I crossed the desert
and left the road behind.

I swear by a god who writes his book
in the caves of ancient torture
I shall lift this fire
and sacrifice a fly.

In the name of every sun that ever comes forth
I call this funeral to order.

To Sisyphus

I swore to write on water.
I swore to help Sisyphus
carry that dumb rock.

I swore to stay with Sisyphus
to submit to fever and to fire,
to search those blind quarries
for one last feather
that will write to grass, to autumn,
the poem of dust.

I swore to live with Sisyphus.

A God Who Loves to Suffer

I say to the god dismembered
in my footsteps—
I am Mihyar, the cursed one.

I offer up the dead in sacrifice.
I pray the prayer of wounded wolves,

except that the graves which yawn in my words
have embraced my songs
with the tight clasp of a god who has removed the stones from us,
who loves his own misery
and blesses even Hell
so he will say my prayers with me
and return innocence to the face of life.

The Spectacle (A Dream)

Just as the thunderbolt interrogated the stones,
it judged the sky.
It judged everything.

Just as history washed itself in my eyes
the days dropped into my hands,
they dropped like fruit.

Winds of Madness

The day's carriages rusted.
So did the knight.

I come from there,
from the country of barren roots,
my horse a wilted bud,
my pathway just a blockade.

So why are you mocking me?
Go away. I'm not from here.

I came to you wrapped in crime,
I brought you these winds of madness.

❧ *You Have No Choice*

What? So you would destroy the face of earth?
You would draw another in its place?

What then? So you have no choice
except the path of fire,
except the hell of denial,

when the whole earth
is a silent executioner's sword,
or a god.

حوار

ـ مَنْ أَنْتَ مِنْ خِئْتُ، يَا مُضْيار؟

أَنَّ أَخْرَجْتَ اللهَ وَهاوِية
الشَّيْطان.

هاوِية تَذْهَبُ وَهاوِية تَجِيءُ،
وَزمانُ لَمْ نَخْتَارُ.

ـ لا اللهَ أُنْثَى وَلا الشَّيْطان
كِلاهُما جِدار،
كِلاهُما يُغْلِقُ لِي عَيْنَيْ،
هَلْ أُبْدِلُ الجِدارَ بالجِدار،
وَحَيْرَتِي مُنيرَة مَنْ يُضِيءُ،
مُنيرَة مَنْ يَعْرِفُ كُلَّ شَيْءٍ.

IV. IRAM OF THE PILLARS

∾ *Psalm*

My country and I tease one another.

I glimpse its future coming forward in the eyelashes of an ostrich, I play around with its history and its great moments, and then I pounce on it, a rock and a thunderbolt. Then, on the other side of the day, I undertake its real history.

To you, there on the other side, I'm a stranger. I inhabit a country all mine.

Asleep and awake I open a bud and climb inside.

There's a need for something to be born. That's why for the lightning I open caves under my skin and build my nests. I need to split the sky, like thunder, to open lips as sad as straw, between stone and the dying season, to get between pores and skin, between one thigh and another.

That's why I sing: "Come forth, you shape tailored to our dying."

That's why I shout singing: "Who else will let us mother a new space, will nourish us with death?"

I make progress towards myself and towards the ruins. Calamity claims me—I am too short to encircle the earth like a rope, and not sharp enough to plunge into the face of history.

You want me to be like you. You want to cook me in the kettle of your prayers, to serve me with the soup of soldiers, the pepper of tyrants. Then you want to pitch me like a tent for the ruler and raise my skull as your flag—

(As for you, my death, in spite of all this I'm running towards you. I run, I run, I run.)

What separates me from you is a distance vast as a mirage.

I stir up the hyenas in you. I stir up the gods. I plant discord in you and feed you to the fever. Later, I'll teach you to walk without a guide. I am the pole to your equator, a springtime let loose. I am the shudder in your throats. In your words there is a bloodletting of my own. You approach me like leprosy. I'm the one tied to your soil. But there is nothing that brings us together, whereas everything that is separates us—so let me burn alone. Let me pass through you as a spear of light.

I cannot live with you. I cannot live without you either. You are the undulation in my senses. There is no escape from you. Go ahead and scream—the sea, the sea—but make sure you hang the beads of the sun upon your thresholds.

Go ahead and reopen up my memory. Take a good look at my face under the words and scrutinize all those letters. When you see the froth that clothes my flesh and the pile of stones flowing in my blood you will see me.

Closed in, like the trunk of a tree, really here, like the air, I can't be grasped. That's why I can't surrender myself to you.

I was born in a lilac's eyelids. I grew up in the orbit of lightning. I live between light and grass. I storm and I wake up. I shine and I cloud over. I rain and I snow—the hours are my language, day my country.

"People are asleep. When they die they will become aware." Or, as has been said: "While you are asleep, if you become aware of it you die." This is how people are going to say it.

You are just smudges on my windowpane. I will have to erase you. I'm the dawning day, the map that draws itself. In spite of that, there's a fever inside me, tending you throughout the night.

Nonetheless I still await you.
In the shells of night along the seashore
in the roar coming from the sea's depths
in the holes that fill the sky's gown
in jujube and acacia,
in pine and cedar,
in the lining of the waves—in their very salt
I wait for you.

∾ *Vision*

I glimpse among submissive books
in a yellow dome
a perforated city flying by.

I glimpse walls fashioned of silk
a murdered star
swimming in a green flask.

I glimpse a statue made of tears
its dismembered limbs made from broken pottery
bowing down before the prince.

City (Voices)

"She bowed down to the smoke, to the smoke.
She floats, a raft on the winds.

Her face, a frog's face. She has two fingers.
She will never touch the tentacles of spring,
never experience the feel of a morning river.

She is the pond where the herd drinks
She has one face, two navels."

Innocence

I accuse the ghosts.
I accuse the rukh who lays her eggs
on the shoulder of a blind genie.

I accuse the winds,
The candles, the mute chicken.
I accuse the winged adder
(what a leprous, broken wing!)—
I accuse the trees and the water.

Because you, our illuminated sky,
wife to the sultan and the god,
you are innocent of our blood, innocent.

Prostitute

We have lips
full of this stupid world,
the remnants of light-bearing corpses.

Our concealed expulsion
from the locked balconies of paradise
still belongs to us.

O Magic, you comforting spell,
we portray you as an atonement,
an adolescent bed for a whoring land.

Spell

You haven't a single artery.
Your skin lives alone and turns on its own,
Plunges into a whirlpool of dry peels.
Your skin grows dry, naked.

Your skin stretches out like words.
It survives inscribed on houses
with sand and marble.

Your days of mange await you
in the pupils of a blind locust
bearing down on you in spider skin.

Two Corpses

It was in your lowly entrails
your head, your eyes and hands,

I buried a minaret.
I buried the two corpses,
earth and sky.

That tribe of ours,
The beetle-infested womb, windmill turned by the breeze.

The Golden Age

—Take him away, Officer.
—Sir, I know the executioner's sword
awaits me,
except that I am a poet.
I worship my fire
and love my Golgotha.

—Take him away, Officer.
Tell him that an officer's shoes
look better than his face.

O age of golden shoes,
you are more precious and more beautiful.

Things

If only I could have traced the wound back to the crime,
could have disguised the flag, its madness,
I would have worn a cap of invisibility—
whether in victory or in defeat,
I would have occupied the dream weighing down my eyelids.
I would have been on earth without really existing.

Instead I linked my face
to things, and to my depths, to God,
happy to live without a magic power,
to sketch life
with the pen of death,
the pen of illusions and of things.

I was satisfied to live with things.

Dress Up in Sand

Dress up in sand, wear wolf's clothing
you woman of the wind from Damascus.
I have no moon, no clothes to offer.
I dared to sleep
in your dead face,
dead like the bay
a face long dedicated to sobbing.

You are a language that anchors in the port of words
without a greeting,
you woman of the wind from Damascus.

The City

Candles snuffed out over my forehead,
candles lit over the city
and the city
a man whose forehead never knew the light.

And the city is a stone receding into the distance,
what is left of a ship.

It May Become My Country

Look at me. I'm rising above my country's morning,
above its ruins, above its highest peaks.
Look at me. I'm ridding myself of death's heavy burden.
Here I am abandoning it in order to see it better.

For tomorrow it may become my country.

For My Land

It is for my land that I bleed these cursed veins.
For its sake I stowed tomorrow and my winds
among my many wounds.

My land knows the future—that amulet.
My land has drunk too much—instead of shoulders,
it has princes, one of pearl, one of crime.

The Rapture of Madness

I have knocked over castles of sand created in my eyes.
I've granted to the monastery
censers of opium—
censers of opium, carpets and mirrors.

I've cursed the face of patience, of consent.
I danced for the stars to set,
for the corpse of some god.

I swear by your name, you cloud of bells
heralding the wedding of ruins and of drought,
by your name, foreheads stained with terror.

Homeland

To faces shrunk under a mask of sadness
I bow down. To the paths where I forgot my tears,
for a father who died green, like a cloud,
a sail still unfurled in his face,
I bow down. To a child who has been sold
so he might pray and shine shoes.
(All of us in my country, we pray. All of us shine shoes.)

And to rocks where my hunger engraved a message:
This rock is really rain rolling under my eyelids, it's lightning.
And I bow down to a house whose soil I carried with me
when I was lost. These all are my homeland. Not Damascus.

Distant Face

When I broke through the crust, that layer of ice,
when I killed the moon, with its covering magic and smoke—
that's when I reached your depths,
illuminated with grass and with innocence.
I brought closer the face of the distant world.

You're not on my bed, blanketed with madness,
you have no sand in your eyes.
You're not with me, with straw, nor with my drought,
you woman of pain, of flint
O sister of Qasiyun.

Voice

More precious than terror,
more than stifled disobedience—
that is you, more precious even than thunder over the desert.

O broken homeland, glued together,
walking beside me with your faltering steps.

Vision

Our city fled
and I ran behind to discover its pathways.
I looked—glimpsed only the horizon.
I saw those who would escape tomorrow
and those who would come back tomorrow
a single body
I tear to pieces on this page.

I saw—that the cloud was a throat.
Water became a wall of flame.
I saw a sticky yellow thread hanging on me,
unraveled from history.
A hand that inherited a race of puppets
and a dynasty of rags loosens a thread,
draws out my own past,
ties it together and feeds it back to history.

I entered into the ritual of creation,
The water's womb, the virginity of trees.
I saw trees seducing me,
but in their branches I saw rooms,
beds, windows, which resisted me.
I saw children. I read to them
my story of the sand,

I read to them the suras of the clouds
and the verses of the stone.
I saw how they traveled along with me.
I saw how pools of tears
and rain that died
shone behind them.

Our city fled—
What am I? What? A wheat stalk crying over a skylark
that died covered by snow and cold?
Our city died without making public
her letters about me.
She didn't write to anyone.
When I saw her corpse lying at the end of time,
I screamed "O silence of ice,
let me be her homeland in her exile.
I am a stranger here. Her grave is my homeland."

Our city fled.
I watched my foot become a river
overflowing with blood,
and boats in the receding distance
fanning out.
I saw my shores as a temptation to drown,
I saw my waves as wind, as swan.

Our city fled.
Rejection was a broken pearl
whose fragments settled on my ships.
Rejection is a woodcutter living on my face.
He gathers me up and lights the pieces.
Rejection is the distances that scatter me
until I see my blood. I see behind my blood
death talking to me, stalking me.

Our city fled.
I saw how my shroud makes me glow.
And I saw. If only death would wait awhile for me.

☙ *Shaddâd*

He's back.
So raise the banner of yearning.
Leave your denial as a sign
on the road of the years,
over these stones
in the name of Iram of the Pillars.

Iram is the homeland of those who deny,
those who wasted their years in despair
who broke the seals on the ancient flasks
and, making light of the warnings,
ignored the bridges of safety.

This is our land, our only inheritance.
We are its children, waiting for Judgment Day.

سَفَر

مُسَافِرٌ دُونَا حِيرَانٌ

يَا شَمْسُ

مِنْ أَيْنَ

لِيَ فِطْابٌ ؟

V. These Petty Times

Psalm

Where do the distances end, where does fear stop?

I call on emptiness, I empty out what is full. Even flint is pliable, even sand takes root in water. Why the roads? Why the arrival?

Lost, totally lost. Nor shall I return. Falling is my natural condition, paradise my contrary.

I am a wedding, and I announce the attraction of death. I am the clouds, I know no drought. I am the wastes without a single cloud.

I hide behind riddles, I hide under the robe of the seasons and peek out from its ripped seams. I give my footsteps their shape and say to the sea follow me.

Trees are the leaves in my notebooks, and the stones poems, like me.

I shall scrape off the horizon's hide until it bleeds. I shall fly from one wound to another.

We divide the sky up, Death and I.

We raise the flag of hunger, Bread and I.

Tomorrow, trapped in the robe of myth, I'll climb the wall of shadow. A procession, songs of stone, will stick to me.

O madness, my master, my messiah.

I search for a sun living in the eyes, for eyes that see the light, all the light. I'm looking for a tree trunk, looking for what gives the word its gender, and for what pierces the skies.

I search for something to give stones the lips of children, and to give history the rainbow, to give songs the throats of trees.

I search for something to extend the rippling limits, limits that cannot be seen between the sea and the rocks, between the clouds and the sand, between the day and night.

I search for something that will harmonize our voices: God and I, Satan and I, the universe and I, something with which to plant discord between us.

You, my search, the container I collect things in.

Day

Day has clothed us in his old robe.

Day has cried over us here and there,
opening his chest to defeat,
casting the angel's sign
over our dismembered bodies,
over our footsteps.

Road

I'm speaking to the road that refuses to begin.
We have but one face, a face that saw,
that loved the day, loved its very existence.

In our land there was a god. When he was away from us we
    forgot him.
Behind him we burned the temple, its candles and its vows.

From that absence you and I fashioned
an idol made of clay.
We stoned him,
we stoned him because we were there,
with the road that almost began.

O road who doesn't know how to begin.

No Words Between Us

Will the sand leave our eyelashes,
will a storm wash this land of its garbage?

You seeds, crumble and burn.
There are no words between us, no echo—
and all the bridges have collapsed
even before the roads.

≈ *Farewell*

Years ago we called you "farewell."
We called you an elegy of regret,
you haloes of dead angels
you, language of locusts in flight.

Words get mired down.
In labor words become more beautiful.

Absent wombs return to us,
and here are the rainstorms and the torrents,
O language of the rubble,
O halo of dead angels.

≈ *Death*

When we create no gods, we die.
When we don't kill them, we die.

Listen, kingdom of lost stone.

≈ *Luminous Winds*

The winds bereft of light, the luminous winds—
are still behind us, approaching slowly.

We walk this road with terror as companion,
with Barada and the Euphrates flowing between us.

How often we have carried them through the wastes,
as a banner of dust, of laurels.
Often we have whispered them as a prayer—
Barada . . . Euphrates . . .

The winds bereft of light, the luminous winds—
are still behind us, approaching slowly.

Shell

The city's face darted through our eyelashes
lost beneath masks of ice.
So we shouted out

"We are alive in the folds of the city
snails behind their shells.

Denial, come find us."

Land of Absence

This is it, the land of torture.
No tomorrow ever arrives.
No wind illuminates us.

Any voice at all might come,
my friends, in this land of absence.

Letter

There was a country we dreamed about.
We opened a road to it, a horizon
that timid eyelids had cut through.
Yesterday in the pride of my friend Madness,
in the passing of childhood,
we hungered for this land. We drew
a picture inspired by its name, its glory.
We wrote it a letter—
"To the country wounded by timid eyelids."

The Lost Ones

For you, the lost and confused,
you who arrived before there was a road,
before there was a call,

it's in your name that the dawn of heaven arrives,
a sorcerer grasping like fire.
This land of ours is for you. For you our beautiful virgins.

It was for you, in these stubborn winds,
this poem was written.
For you, the lost and confused.

Loss

Loss, loss.
Loss saves us. It guides our footsteps.
And loss is a radiance.
All else a mask.

Loss unifies us with something other than us.
And loss fastens the face of the sea
to our dreaming.

And loss is just waiting.

The Sun Returns

Fate shook itself out over the seas.
Superstition broke its seal.
Here are the lowlands.
Enable us to plant the shores with oysters,
to anchor the Ark on Mt. Sannîn.
Enable us to slay the dragon,
O master of superstition.

When the bells toll and the road
laments the sun's exile from the city
wake up for us, you thunderous flame behind the hills—
wake up, Phoenix—

so we can welcome the vision of his sad fire
before the dawn, before it's all been said.
We'll carry his eyes along the road
celebrating the sun's return to the city.

The Stone in Love

The journey is over. The road
is a stone in love.

Here we are burying the slaughtered day
dressed in the winds of tragedy.
Come morning we'll shake the date palms again.

Tomorrow we'll wash the emaciated god
with blood from thunderbolts.
We'll extend slender threads
between our eyelids and the road.

Flags

Those threads woven by roots
between our eyelashes and the dust
are weighed down with the day's remnants
weighed down by bridges—

those threads, our flags in the journey of dust.

Flood

Go away, Dove. We don't want you to return.

They have delivered their flesh to the rocks,
and as for me—I edge ever closer towards the bottomless pit,
dangling from the ship's sail.

Our flood is a planet anchored in place.
It is an ancient waste.
Perhaps we'll inhale the scent of a god from buried time.

Go away, Dove. We don't want you to return.

These Petty Times

The false mirage is ours. The blind day
and the guide's corpse are also ours.
We are the generation of the ship.
We are the generation of this contemptible time.

The safe seas delivered us,
Those seas that sing the elegy of departure,
they delivered us into the labyrinth.

We are the generation of endless dialogue
between our ruins and the god.

City

Our fire edges closer to the city,
to dismantle its bed.

We shall dismantle the city's bed.
We shall live and, dodging arrows, cross over,
towards the land of bewildered clarity,
even behind that mask stuck to this orbiting rock,
around the whirlpool of terror,
around the echo, and around words.
And we shall wash clean the day's insides,
its intestines, the unborn life inside,
and in the city's name we shall burn that tattered existence.
We shall reverse the face of its presence
and make the city reveal the distances made close.

Our fire advances. The grass is born in the rebellious ember.
Our fire edges over towards the city.

موت

تموت اِن لَم تَخلُق الآلِهة

تموت اِن لَم تَفضُل الآلِهة

يا مَلَكوت الصَّخرة التائهة

VI. Edge of the World

✎ Psalm

I create a chest for the wind and a waist to lean up against. I create a face for rejection to wear and I compare it with my own. I take the clouds for notebooks and for ink and wash the light clean.

I wear the elegance of anemones. The pine tree has a waist that smiles for me. I find no one to love. But will Death hold it against me that I love myself?

I devise a kind of water that doesn't quench my thirst. I'm like the air—there's no law for me. I create a climate where heaven and hell overlap. I invent other devils. I race and we place bets on things.

In my dust cloud eyes are swept up. I steal into the fibers of the past, reopening the memory of those who came before. I weave their colors and color the needles that sew them. Once worn out I rest in the blueness, and all at once my labor rises, a sun, and glows, a moon.

I set earth free and imprison the skies. I fall down in order to stay faithful to the light, in order to make the world ambiguous, fascinating, changeable, dangerous, in order to announce the steps beyond.

The blood of the gods is still fresh on my clothes. A seagull's scream echoes through my pages. So let me just pack up my words and leave.

✎ Journey

A traveler stuck in place:
How, O Sun, could I ever claim your steps?

✎ Edge of the World

What do I care about the possible—whether happy or in pain?
In my hymns I write my own bible.
I look for a place to hide,
for a world that starts at the edge of this world.

Adam

Adam whispered to me,
an oh of pain choking silently in him—
"I'm not the father of the world.
I've never glimpsed paradise.
Take me to God."

Island of Stone

An island, all stone
and sparks,
takes shape around my footsteps.

Its waves have settled here,
but its coastline journeys on.

Crow's Feather

I.
Coming without a flower, without a field.
Coming without seasons.

There is nothing for me in the sands or in the winds
in the glory of the morning
except fresh blood
flowing along with the sky.
The earth I wear prophetic on my forehead
stretches endlessly across the sky.

Coming without seasons
coming with a flower, without a field,

in my blood a spring of dust wells up.
I'm living in my eyes,
eating from my eyes.

Living, I suffer the years, waiting
for a ship to embrace the here and now
as it plunges to the depths,
as if dreaming or just unsure,
sailing off never to come back.

II.
In the cancer of silence, under siege,
I write these poems on the soil
with a crow's feather.
I know too well no light shines on my eyelids—
nothing except the wisdom of dust.

I sit in the coffeehouse. My companions, day,
the wood of this chair,
and these discarded cigarette butts.
I sit here awaiting
my forgotten appointment.

III.
I want to kneel down in prayer
for the broken winged owl,
for the embers and the winds.
I want to pray
for the planet perplexed in the sky,
for death, for disease.
I want my incense to consume
my blank days, my songs,
my notebook, ink and inkwell.
I want to pray
for anything that knows no prayer.

IV.

Beirut did not appear on my route.
It never flowered. These are my fields.
Beirut never bore fruit.
And this is the spring of locusts and of sand
covering my fields.
I'm alone without a flower, without a season,
alone with the fruits.
From sunset to dawn
Never seeing Beirut, I keep crossing it.
I live in Beirut without seeing it.

I'm alone with love and with fruit.
We walk with day for a companion,
then leave for another place.

Dawn Cuts Its Own Thread

Dawn cuts its own thread,
lays its eyelids on the soil.
My hands two masts clasping
the sails of sunset.

My windows are gone.
There are no flowers left, not a book to be found,
just me and the corners.
I have my own slender threads, my own crow.

The Door

For weeks now his eyelids
have been lurking at the door.
His body, lost in bed.

He searches, heart at the door.
There is no hand that knocks.

He feels the urge to cry.
"How precious crying is, how valuable.
Down this river of tears
comes a ship bearing my loved ones."

❧ *Who Are You?*

A butterfly has my eyes
and terror afflicts my songs.

"Who are you?"
"A lost spear,
a god who survives without prayer."

❧ *The New Noah*

I.
We went with the Ark, our oars
a promise from God, under rain
and in mud we live while people die.
We went with the waves. Space was
a rope formed of corpses, connecting
our years to theirs. There was between sky
and us a window for supplication:

"O Lord, why did you save only us
among all the people, all the living things?
Where will you throw us? In your other land?
In our original home?
In the leaves of death, in the wind of life?

O Lord, there is inside us, in our arteries
a fear of the sun. We've given up on light,
we're tired of all these tomorrows,
of reliving our years from the start.

If only we had not become this seed
for creation, for the earth and its generations.
If only we were still just clay.
Or an ember, or still in the between,
in order not to see this world, not to see
its hell and its god twice over."

II.

If the original time were to return,
and water again covered the face of life,
if the earth shook and God rushed
to tell me, "Noah, save the living
for Us"—I'd pay no attention to God's words.
I'd go enter the Ark
only to remove pebbles and clay
from the eye sockets of the dead,
and open them to the flood,
to whisper in their veins that we
have come back from being lost,
have come out of that cave,
have lengthened the scope of years
and that we sail unafraid,
not heeding what God says.

Our appointment is with death,
our shores a despair we're used to.
We're satisfied that it is
an ocean of ice, with water hard as steel.
We traverse it to the end.
We sail on without listening to that god,
we who yearned for a new lord.

VII. Persistent Death

Elegy Without Death

Homeland behind bars:
I'm running after it
through a forest of weddings,
through a childhood of bells.

I'm enlisting eyelashes, calling forth the doubts
who stand in attendance
around this bed of grass and harvest.
I'm saddling the horses,
aiming towards my country,
homeland where ice has gathered on eyelids.

Elegy for Omar ibn al-Khattâb

Without promise, without pretense,
A voice calls out. The sun is his umbrella.
When, oh when will your nature catch up with you?

Friend of despair, of hope,
green stone suspended over the fire,
we're awaiting
your encounter with the sky.

Elegy for Abu Nuwâs

The day around you just a world of ruins,
wanderer, poet charging out of history
into the face of his own time,
know that behind you in the stony procession
through our dead history

stand poetry, the rain, and I.
For my pen, the breasts of tavern maids. For my pages, life itself.

Abu Nuwâs, let's resign ourselves
to the evenings that wrap their cloak around us.
Resign ourselves to those old ruins.
Our loved ones are our tyrants, deceitful as the sky.
Leave us to the torture of beauty, to the wind and its sparks.
Let's do away with rebirth and with hope.
Let us sing, cry out for help, living along with the stone,
with poetry, the rain, and us.

Abu Nuwâs, let's just resign ourselves.

Elegy for al-Hallâj

Your green poisoned plume,
its cheeks swelling with flame,
the star beckoning from Baghdad,
this is our history, our imminent rebirth
in this land of ours—in our persistent death.

Time has lounged in your arms.
From your eyes an all-consuming fire
extends to the sky.

Star shining from Baghdad
loaded with poetry, charged with new birth,
green, poisoned plume.

Nothing remains for those coming from afar,
coming with echoes, bearing death and ice
into this land of rebirth.
Nothing remains for them except your looming presence,

you language of Galilean thunder
in this superficial land,
poet of secrets, poet sprouting roots.

Elegy for Bashshâr

Don't cry over him. Leave him to the whims of the mad caliph.
Call him the devil. Call him the plague.
He's still here with us
rumbling through unhearing streets,
rumbling through our muted depths,
rumbling like an earthquake.

And he is here with us,
still blind, with no land, no city,
searching for a blue pearl.
His faithful poems will preserve it
for the lean year.

Elegy

You, dead on the cross,
my friend,
the roadside flowers have mirrored your face.
A threshold opens up behind your footsteps.

Elegy

Dust sings you, offering you its poems.
To the precipice it gives your footsteps.
and elegizes what remains
of your songs, your vision.

Dust, gathering on the seasons' windowpanes,
covers the mirrors
and collects on your hands.

19: The Arabic text of the epigraph is not a translation, but a loose paraphrase of a poem by Friedrich Hölderlin, "Warum, o schöne Sonne":

> Warum, o schöne Sonne, genügst du mir
> Du Blüte meiner Blüten! am Maitag nicht?
> Was weiß ich höhers denn?
> O daß ich lieber ware, wie Kinder sind!
> Daß ich, wie Nachtigallen, ein sorglos Lied
> Von meiner Wonne sänge!

23: "Psalm": "He creates his own kind. Starting with himself. He has no ancestors. His roots are in his footsteps." (*Yakhluqu naw'ahu min nafsihi—lâ aslâfa lahu wa fî khatawâtihi judhûruhu.*) This is the text running along the bottom of Kamal Boullata's cover for this book.

31–32: In the 1961 edition, the following poem appeared between "Day's Twin" and "The Others":

The Winds of Day

> What's wrong with you?
> Mihyar is lost. He has unraveled
> all his riddles, thrown them away,
> a stone in the book of dust.
>
> Go ahead, lift sail.
> Travel across the seas.
> Don't you see other oceans looming?
> What's wrong with you?
> The winds of day have pulled ahead of you.

75: The phrase "Iram of the Pillars" (*Iram dhât al-'imâd*), the legendary city of the people of 'Âd, occurs in the Qur'ân (89.7) in a list of ancient cultures now gone, with the ancient Egyptians and Thamûd.

78: "Psalm": "People are asleep. When they die they will become aware." The proverbial statement is attributed to Ali, the Prophet's nephew.

79: "City (Voices)": In the Arabic text the entire poem is printed between quotation marks.

84: "Homeland": The phrase "for a father who died green, like a cloud, / a sail still unfurled in his face" (*li-abin mâta akhdara ka-s-sahâba / wa 'alâ wajhi-hi shirâ'u*) is represented in the vertical calligraphy on Kamal Boullata's cover for this book.

84: "Distant Face": Qasiyun (near Damascus) is where the great mystical philosopher Ibn al-'Arabi (1165–1240 AD) is buried.

87: Shaddâd is the name of the mythical figure thought to have designed the city of Iram.

109–111: Omar ibn al-Khattâb was the second leader (r. 634–644 AD) of the Islamic community after the death of the Prophet Muhammad.

Abu Nuwâs (d. 810 AD) was famous in Baghdad during the reign of Hârûn al-Rashîd as an innovative poet, known particularly for his poems celebrating wine.

Al-Hallâj, an early Sufi figure, was executed in Baghdad in 922 AD for blasphemy. (His crime was the mystical statement *"Anâ al-haqq,"* "I am the Truth.")

Bashshâr ibn Burd (714–784 AD), blind from birth, became one of the most respected early innovators among the poets of the Abbasid period.

❧ Acknowledgments

Translations from this collection, some in earlier versions, have appeared in the following periodicals:

Guernica: A Magazine of Art and Politics: "Mask of Songs," "In the City of the Partisans," "New Testament";

Jusoor: "The Wound," "The Loss," "Stone," "The Fall," "Dialogue," "The Dialect of Sin," "King over the Winds," and the psalms that begin the sections entitled "The Knight of Strange Words" and "The Sorcerer of Dust";

Literature East and West: "Neither a Star," "In the City of the Partisans";

The New Yorker: "Chair (A Dream)," "Homeland."

A grant from The Rockefeller Foundation for residency at the Bellagio Study and Conference Center in Italy allowed the translators full-time collaboration in November 2006. An earlier travel grant from the University of North Dakota likewise allowed a period of collaboration towards the beginning of the project. Particular thanks go to Robin Magowan for a thorough rhythm transplant, which we hope has survived, and which we hope he will recognize in the final version of these poems; to Pilar Palaciá, the managing director at Bellagio for her hospitality; to Paula whose technical advice manifested itself when we needed it most; to Victoria for being there; to Adonis for his trust in us.

❧

✍ *About the Author*

Adonis, pen name of Ali Ahmad Saʻid (b. 1930), is perhaps the most accomplished, inventive, and widely respected contemporary Arab poet. He has been a shaping force in Arabic poetry at least since 1956, when he was a founding editor of the Lebanese magazine *Shi'r* (Poetry) and later *Mawâqif* (Positions, founded in 1968), exerting a profound influence not only as a practitioner but also as an editor and critic. He has been recognized for his poetry often, most recently with the Bjørnson prize from the Bjørnstjerne Bjørnson Academy in Molde, Norway. Among his most important contributions to the lyric tradition in Arabic are *Kitâb al-Tahawwulât wa al-hijra fi aqâlîm al-nahâr wa al-layl* (The book of metamorphoses and migration in the regions of day and night, 1965), which resembles the Mihyar poems in its aesthetic compactness; *Waqt bayna al-ramâd wa al-ward* (1970), translated by Shawkat M. Toorawa as *A Time Between Ashes and Roses* (2004), poems that combine a surrealist energy with political commentary; *Mufrad bi-sîghat al-jam'* (Singular in the form of plural, 1975, revised 1988), which opens a whole other direction with visual effects that position words surprisingly on the blank page; and the two volumes of *Al-Kitâb* (The book, 1995 and 1998). The collection translated here, *Aghânî Mihyâr al-Dimashqî* (1961), is the earliest of his many lyrical manifestoes.

✍

❧ About the Translators

Adnan Haydar is head of the Arabic section in the Department of Foreign Languages and professor of Arabic and comparative literature at the University of Arkansas, where he also directed the King Fahd Middle East Studies Program from 1993 to 1999. His books include translations of Jabra Ibrahim Jabra's *The Ship* and *In Search of Walid Masoud* (with Roger Allen).

Michael Beard teaches in the English Department at the University of North Dakota. He is the author of a book on the Iranian writer Sadeq Hedayat, *Hedayat's Blind Owl and the West* (1990), and more recently has translated from Persian two volumes of short poems by Abbas Kiarostami, *Walking with the Wind* (with Ahmad Karimi-Hakkak, 2001) and *A Wolf Lying in Wait / Gorgi dar kamin* (with the late Karim Emami, 2005).

Haydar and Beard have collaborated frequently: on an edited collection of literary essays *Naguib Mahfouz: From Regional Fame to Global Recognition* (1993) and on numerous translations of Arabic poetry, including Khalil Hawi's *Naked in Exile* (1983) and Henri Zoghaib's *In Forbidden Time* (1991). They work together as coeditors of The Middle East Translation Series for Syracuse University Press.

❧

The Lannan Translations Selection Series

Ljuba Merlina Bortolani, *The Siege*

Olga Orozco, *Engravings Torn from Insomnia*

Gérard Martin, *The Hiddenness of the World*

Fadhil Al-Azzawi, *Miracle Maker*

Sándor Csoóri, *Before and After the Fall: New Poems*

Francisca Aguirre, *Ithaca*

Jean-Michel Maulpoix, *A Matter of Blue*

Willow, Wine, Mirror, Moon:
Women's Poems from Tang China

Felipe Benítez Reyes, *Probable Lives*

Ko Un, *Flowers of a Moment*

Paulo Henriques Britto, *The Clean Shirt of It*

Moikom Zeqo, *I Don't Believe in Ghosts*

Adonis (Ali Ahmad Saʻid), *Mihyar of Damascus, His Songs*

For more on the Lannan Translations Selection Series
visit our Web site:
www.boaeditions.org

Printed in the USA
CPSIA information can be obtained
at www.ICGtesting.com
JSHW082220140824
68134JS00015B/653